The TLC Manual

A tender loving care instructional for the little light within you.

by Susan Catherine Collyer

The Lightworks Press
susanccollyer@aol.com

For my son Matthew

Have you ever introduced yourself
to the smallest part
of you?

hello!

This little self is called, A Light Baby!

THIS DELIGHTFUL SELF,
PERHAPS HIDDEN BY A FEW GRAY HAIRS, A
FEW POUNDS, A FEW FEARS OR TEARS............

IS STILL HERE!!

JUST HANGIN' OUT IN YOUR HEART, WAITING FOR YOU TO COME AND PLAY.

PERHAPS YOUR LITTLE ONE IS...

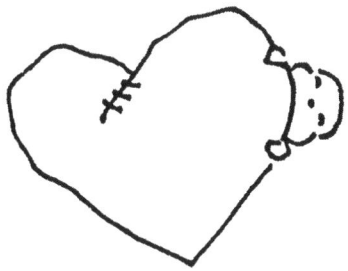

HIDING?

UNDER THE BIG GROWN UP WORDS LIKE:
        RATIONALITY
        REASON..
        RIDICULOUS!!!

        . . . . . . WE CONCUR.

The 'R' words are important, of course. You would never, for instance, wish to release your little sparkle in an office during a VIP management meeting and perhaps --stick pencils up your nose because you're really bored and have to pretend to be rapt with attention.

NO.
COMPLETELY INAPPROPRIATE.
Therefore, we suggest doing these exercises in private, daily, until you and your little one feel more comfortable with such wild expressions of freedom.

THE DAILY EXERCISES.

a light weight

CAUTION WARNING!

THESE ARE REALLY VERY SILLY.

THEY MAY CAUSE EMBARASSMENT, JUDGEMENT, DISDAIN, ARROGANCE OR SOME FATAL FORM OF:
"OH REALLY! GET REAL.. NOT IN MY LIFETIME.."
"YEAH, WHATEVER"

THIS IS ACTUALLY VERY LETHAL TO THE INTOXICATING EXPERIENCE OF DELIGHT AND INNOCENCE.

FOR BEST RESULTS DO THESE EXERCISES EACH DAY FOR A LOVELY CUMULATIVE EFFECT.
PROCEED AT RISK TO CRITIC WITHIN

1. A KISS

ADMINISTERED TO ONES' OWN HAND, ARM... FOOT, TOE (IF YOU CAN REACH IT), SHOULDER OR ANY OTHER DELIGHTFULLY, REACHABLE, NEEDY PART.

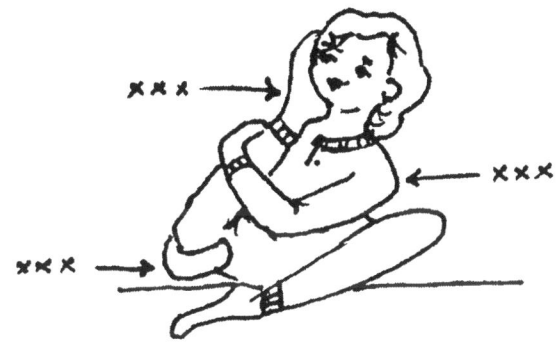

BE CREATIVE
GOOD LUCK

2. A WORD OR TWO.

LOVING WORDS OF APPROVAL, ACCEPTANCE, ENCOURAGEMENT OR EVEN PRAISE SUCH AS:

> "YOU ARE REALLY SOMETHIN' SPECIAL"
> "YOU'RE TRULY EXCEPTIONAL AND MAGNIFICENT!"
> REPEATING SEVERAL TIMES: "YOU ARE SO COOL!!!"
> ......IS A GREAT BEGINNING.

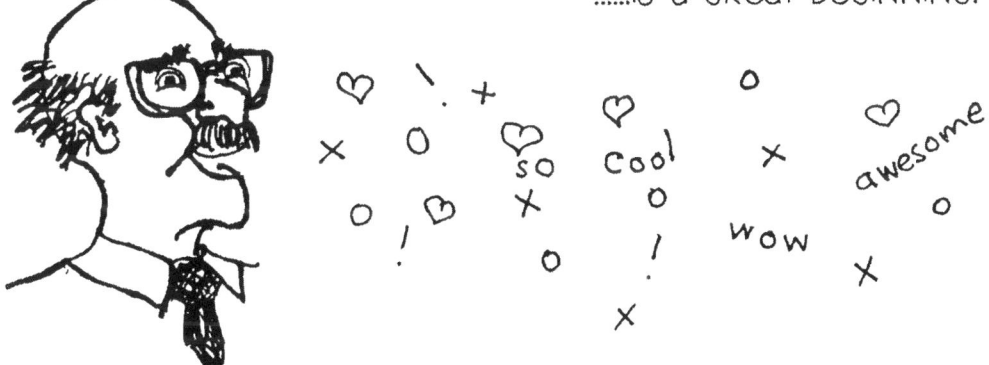

ADDING "<u>NO MATTER WHAT</u>" IS AN EXCELLENT POSTSCRIPT FOR ALL OF THE ABOVE

3. A TOUCH.

(OK, THIS IS MORE ADVANCED)
A CARING LIGHT STROKE TO YOUR CHEEK,
FOREHEAD OR SHOULDER DOES WONDERS!!

GIVING A GOOD SQUEEZE
IS OFF THE CHARTS!
WOW.

4. A SMILE.
(OK, WE ARE HEADING TOWARD THE FAMOUS "R" TERRITORY)

BEST ATTEMPTED IN FRONT OF A MIRROR, (FOR FULL EFFECT) BUT WHEN ONE IS NOT AVAILABLE, THE EFFECT IS STILL SIMPLY MARVELOUSLY SILLY.
CAUTION: IF SMILE IS TOO WIDE, YOU MAY BURST INTO NERVOUS SARCASTIC LAUGHTER ie:

5. A LOOK
(TO BE DONE ONLY IN FRONT OF A MIRROR)

A LOOK OF "I SEE YOU, YOU IRRESISTABLE YUM YUM YOU!" OR... "I AM HERE FOR YOU"... OR PERHAPS A SIMPLE "HELLO BEAUTY!" WILL BRING ABOUT THE DESIRED RESULT.

7. HOT/WARM BATH
(seasonally appropriate)

Lavishly administered
with numerous toys available:
ducks, froggies, animal
shaped spongies, soap fishies
small cars, trucks plastic building blocks
and most importantly of all:

BUBBLES!

8. CRAYOLAS & PAPER
really.

CRAYOLAS! THE KIND YOU <u>USED</u> TO HAVE. YES, THE STORES STILL CARRY THEM. BUY A BOX. PUT YOUR NAME ON IT. THESE ARE YOURS. PUT THEM ON YOUR DESK OR IN THE KITCHEN.. SO THEY ARE AVAILABLE. LET THE BOX LURE YOU TO SCRIBBLE, COPY, EXPERIMENT... DRAW ORANGE SKIES, BLUE TREES OR JUST A RED HEART. DRAW WITH THE HAND THAT DOESN'T GET TO DRAW MUCH.

BE OPEN.. AND GENTLE.
THERE LIVES A VULNERABLE AND TENDER SOUL WITHIN.

9. READ A STORY.

PICK OUT YOUR ALL TIME FAVORITEST FAVORITE TALE THEN GO TO THE LIBRARY (REMEMBER DOING THAT?) OR THE BOOKSTORE AND GET A FEW ... PUT THEM NEAR YOUR BED.. AND AT NIGHTIME OR NAPTIME.. READ A LITTLE OUT LOUD.

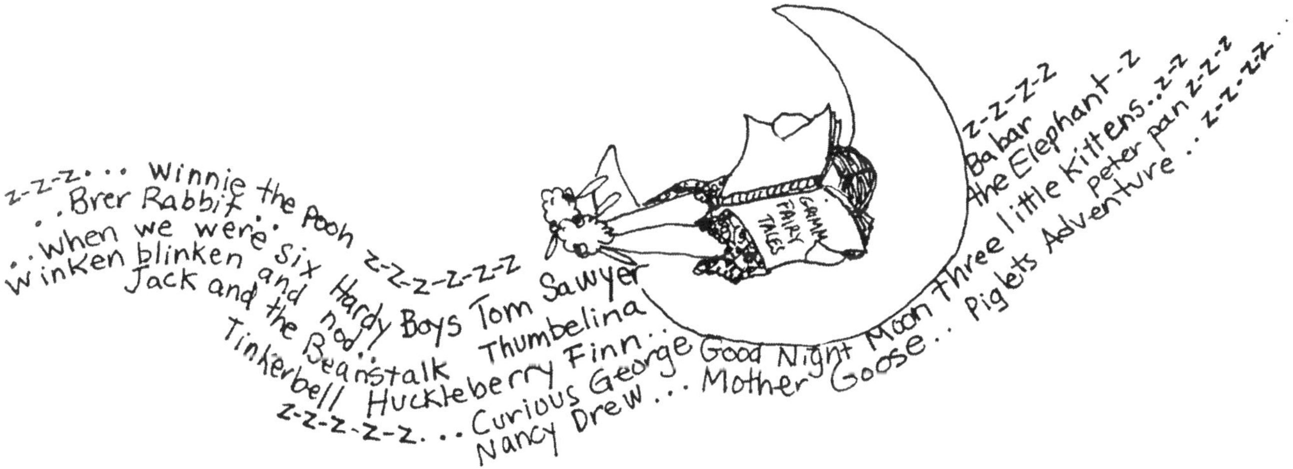
GRIMM FAIRY TALES
z-z-z... Winnie the Pooh z-z-z-z-z-z
..Brer Rabbit..
..When we were Six Hardy Boys Tom Sawyer
Winken blinken and nod!
Jack and the Beanstalk Thumbelina
Tinkerbell Huckleberry Finn...
z-z-z-z-z... Curious George Good Night Moon Three little Kittens..z-z
Nancy Drew... Mother Goose.. Piglets Adventure..z-z-z-z..
z-z-z-z
Babar
the Elephant-z
peter pan z-z-z

OR

IF ALL OF THE AFOREMENTIONED HERETOWITH ABOVE EXERCISES ARE TOO DIFFICULT TO ACTUALIZE, PERHAPS FOLLOWING THE FOLLOWING WILL HELP ASSIST YOU IN COMING OUT OF HIDING.....BECAUSE IF YOU'RE HAVING DIFFICULTY COPING WITH THE MERE THOUGHT OF KISSING YOUR TOES OR BLOWING BUBBLES, THEN WE MUST CONCLUDE THAT THE SILLINESS WITHIN YOU HAS GONE INTO A TEMPORARY HIDING PLACE,

THEREFORE

YOU MAY BUILD ANOTHER HIDING PLACE FOR THE BOTH OF YOU (YOU AND YOU) SO YOU CAN AT LEAST HIDE TOGETHER.

A. A TENT!

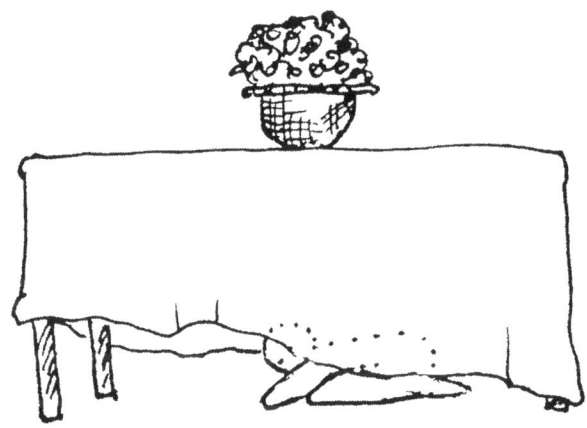

A SHEET OVER A TABLE IS SUPERB.
OR
IF THE SHEET IS NOT YOURS, PLEASE ASK PERMISSION BEFORE DOING THE FOLLOWING.

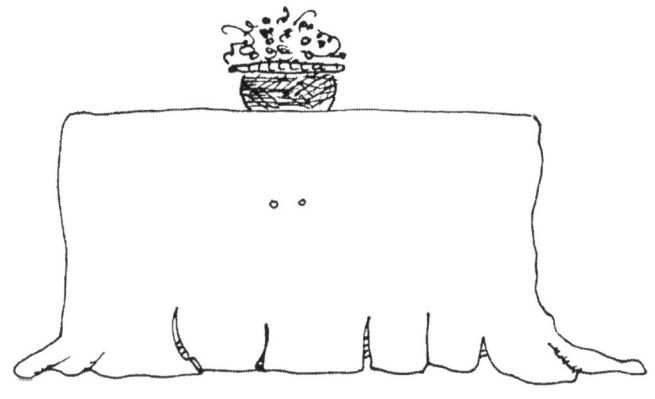

CUT TWO TEENYWEENY
UNNOTICEABLE HOLES- SO YOU CAN SEE OUT
BUT THEY CAN'T SEE YOU!

C. IN THE CUPBOARD!

YOU MAY NEED TO ALSO EMPTY THE CUPBOARD FIRST BEFORE ATTEMPTING TO SQUISH YOURSELF INTO SUCH SPACES.. AND ONCE AGAIN HIDE THE CONTENTS. UNLESS YOU LIVE ALONE OR WISH TO BE FOUND! (OFTEN VERY FUN)

D. Stack Storage Boxes.

Make a small house. Then drape a towel between the stacks for a flexible roof and door.

It's usually a quiet place like an attic, garage or basement. Good for meditations.

e. UNDER THE BED

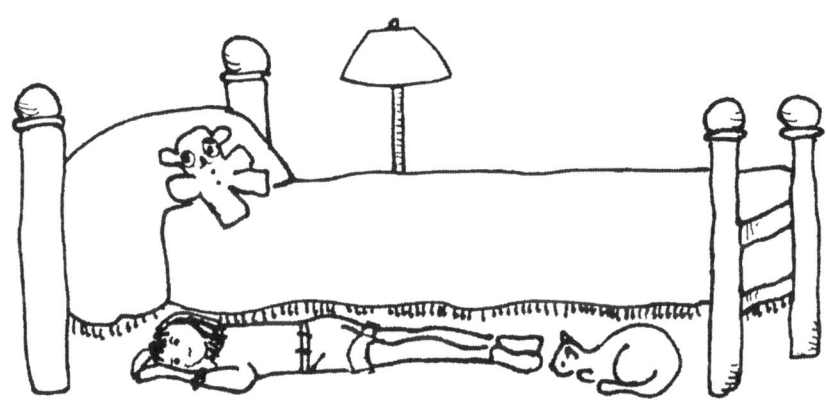

UNLESS IT'S ALREADY OCCUPIED AND YOU WISH TO BE ALONE.

F. a backyard.

try the bushes.

or.........................perhaps.........

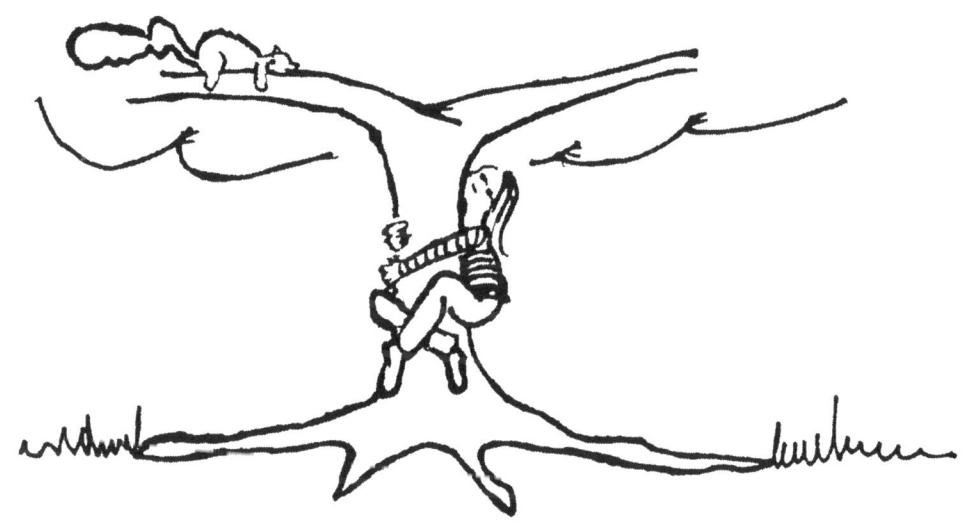

AND IF ANY OF THE PREVIOUS AFOREMENTIONED PARTICULARS AREN'T QUITE WHAT THE DOCTOR ORDERED, PLEASE FOLLOW YOUR OWN INNER DIRECTION.

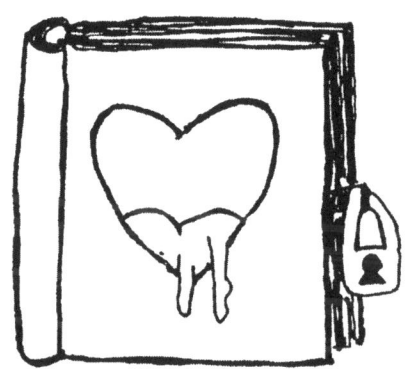

ANY PLACE THAT IS QUIET DARK AND ENCLOSED.
SOFTNESS IS ESPECIALLY HELPFUL.

create a solitary
safe little space
for your inner vulnerable self
to venture forth to be, to think, to feel itself again.

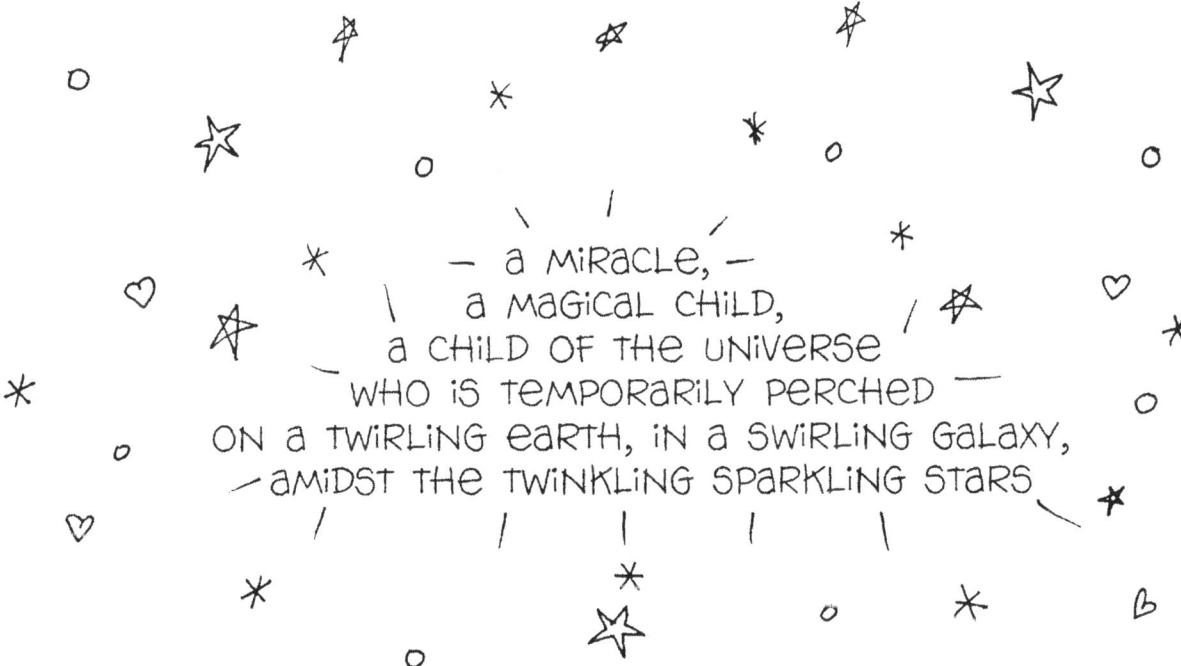

the end……… ❤

*within all darkness lives the light
for the light can never leave us.
within all endings live beginnings,
within all pain, lives Love.*

The Story of the Light Babies™

I was living in a tiny room in NJ, in 1983, working two jobs and commuting to New York City before dawn. I bussed through the Lincoln Tunnel, to the Port Authority tunnels of the subway, to a basement office. I finished after the sunset to go to my night job. I rarely saw daylight. I became deeply depressed and turned to God for help. Why was I alive, what was this all for? I cried myself to sleep. It was my dark night of the soul.

When I awakened the next morning, I was given a Gift. Everything shimmered with light. The sidewalks, the lamposts, the grass and even the tunnels and cars!! I was shown that inside of everything and everyone, there is a GREAT light, that is ALWAYS there, even when we don't see it.

"Don't hide your light but set it high for all to see".
So don't be afraid to let your light shine.

Susan writes and illustrates books which captivate the healing journey.

She believes that art carries the magic of the inner world and transforms the outer world by its power.

Heartfelt thanks to my dear friends Nancy Lester DuTertre, Rodger Parsons, Rosemary Calderalo, Regina Clarkin, Kitty Moynahan, Jim Mulry, Dave Perluck and my beloved late husband, Michael Collyer without whose faith and love this would not have evolved. Special hugs to Sophie and Matthew and all my clients whose healings have healed me.

The Lightworks Press
susanccollyer@aol.com

Made in the USA
San Bernardino, CA
25 September 2014